British Columbia

British Columbia

Featuring British Columbia Photographers

Text by Ted Wrinkle

Published by
Beautiful West Publishing Company
202 N.W. 21st Avenue
Portland, Oregon 97202
and
Whitecap Books, Ltd.
2229 Jefferson Avenue
West Vancouver, B. C., V7V 2A9

First Edition

ISBN 0-915796-43-0 (paperback)
ISBN 0-915796-44-9 (hardbound)
Printed in the United States of America

BEAUTIFUL WEST PUBLISHING COMPANY

CURRENT BOOKS
Mt. Hood, Montana, Utah, Oregon, Washington, California,
Northern California, Colorado, Hawaii, Alaska, Western Impressions,
California Missions, San Francisco, Oregon Coast, British Columbia

FORTHCOMING BOOKS
Maryland, Georgia, New York, Virginia, Arizona, New Mexico,
Lewis and Clark Country, Sierra Nevada, Southern California, Mexico,
Michigan, Texas, Vermont

Send for Complete Catalog, 50c

Beautiful West Publishing Company
202 N. W. 21st Avenue, Portland, Oregon 97209

PHOTO CREDITS

CONTENTS

CREDITS

Lithography by Fremont Litho Inc., Fremont, California

INTRODUCTION

A magnificent coast land of dense rain forests and glaciered mountains, British Columbia is the symbol and reality of wilderness. One of the realities is the monumental scope of the land's natural features. Granite alpine peaks, arid deserts, and crashing river cataracts sweep northward to the Alaska and Yukon borders in a primitive, wild spectacle that has filled human observers with awe, from the early explorers to modern man.

Much of the terrain is formidable, inaccessible: large areas are remote, isolated, and exceptionally rugged. A plane can fly five hundred miles in a straight line and never come upon a single sign of human habitation. Even near major urban centers, alpine wilderness is less than a half hour's travel away. High peaks frame the cities and shelter interior towns from Arctic winds; in British Columbia, the land shapes the people and culture, and the people carefully preserve the land.

Living in natural accommodation with their surroundings, British Columbians have developed a fine sense of environmental awareness. Outdoor recreationalists treat their camping and fishing areas with affection, respect, and a notable concern for the preservation of wilderness. Through their first-hand involvement with nature, these people have learned to recognize the subtle balances of an ecosystem, and man's proper form of participation in it. Practical natural realities sometimes reinforce the value of awareness: local residents can identify grizzly bears and avalanche areas at great visual distances. Yet, it is really the basic relationship to the land that fosters environmental perception.

We know that the preservation of wilderness has not always been the concern of industry. Not very long ago, large tracts of land in southern B. C. were misused, mismanaged, and environmentally debased by commercial interests locked in fierce competition within the forest industry. The areas particularly hard hit by rapine clear-cutting were heavily forested southeast mountain slopes, with the attendant destruction of river salmon spawning beds by logging road construction.

However, for more than a decade now, an enlightened group of representatives from the forest industry, the B. C. Forest Service, and environmentalists of international stature have been working cooperatively to accomplish the most dramatic changes ever witnessed within wood harvesting. The planting of seedlings (near-perfect, fast-growth trees) is the basis of this astonishingly successful attempt to save the southern environment. Most harvesting occurs on government-designated tree farm license lands, with comprehensive on-site inspection by professional environmentalists; and the entire area is replanted on completion. With harvesting being carried out in strictly limited areas, logging has now become a tree-farming resource industry with a new crop every 25 years. More than 100 million seedlings are planted each year, and there are now more trees in the province than at any time before.

The natural character of this land, and its effect on local residents, is the primary reason for the effectiveness of the protective measures that have been taken. British Columbians treasure the values of the wilderness experience, and are determined to preserve their rich natural heritage.

British Columbia is a uniquely north-coast land. Vast areas are primitive wilderness, uncharted, and without roads or any form of access. As in any very large and sparsely populated land, people here characteristically identify with their own specific region. Each region, geographically unique, predetermines a certain way of life. For example, the Cariboo-Chilcotin region immediately evokes images of vast, rolling landscape, and a difficult, frontier existence. A regional approach to British Columbia not only helps gain an understanding of this vast province, it accurately reflects the character of the people and the geography.

In many respects, the future of British Columbia is the future of the natural world. Both the recent advances in environmental protection and the enlightened, educated awareness of individuals augur well for this future. With careful optimism, we can hope that in British Columbia the wilderness will be preserved forever.

(First Preceding Page:) White water dances around rock, outcroppings in Englishman River Canyon, near Port Alberni, Vancouver Island.

(Opposite:) The tide smashes into a rocky shelf near Port Renfrew, on the west coast of Vancouver Island.

(Right:) A glacier lily paints a flash of brilliant color on the forest scene.

(Below:) The craggy Border Peaks stand on the Canada-U.S. border about 70 miles east of Vancouver, B.C. Part of the Skagit Range, they carry glaciers 200 to 300 feet thick on their north slopes.

(Preceding Full Page:) A crescent moon appears tiny and ephemeral hanging over the colossal rock mass of Squamish Chieftain, near Squamish.

(Preceding Page, Above:) Autumn in ranch country brings brilliant gold coloration to an aspen grove near Thalia, southwest of Merritt.

(Preceding Page, Lower:) This idyllic scene combining mountains, sky, and water was photographed at Columbia Lake, headwaters of the Columbia River.

(Left:) A handsome specimen of the wolf tribe poses obligingly for his portrait.

(Below:) A group of snags provide a centerpiece for thi lakeside scene in the Penticton area.

(Opposite:) Some of British Columbia's ranching coun is shown in this sweeping panorama at Riske Creek, gateway to the Chilcotin country.

(Preceding Two Pages:) A clear, rushing forest stream flows over and around the boulders in its bed, meanwhile creating an ideal environment for a variety of Skagit Valley greenery.

(Opposite:) Azouzetta Lake, seen from Pine Pass on the Hart Highway, is in the Peace River district of British Columbia.

(Right:) The exotic-looking skunk cabbage grows in bogs and wet places. Its leaves, up to three feet long, are the largest of any native Canadian plant and its musky smell is similar to that of its namesake. This specimen is on Kanaka Creek, near Haney.

(Lower:) An old cabin basks in soft sunlight in a forested setting on Pender Island, in the Gulf Islands.

(Following Page, Above:) Wapta Mountain pushes its stark bulk out of the surrounding forest in Yoho National Park.

(Following Page, Below:) Autumn brings ''Squamish Gold'' to Squamish Valley.

(Previous Page, Above:) The ubiquitous sword fern thrives in a rain forest of the Coast Range.

(Previous Page, Below:) The rugged peaks of the Vermillion Range lend a wintry backdrop to this lakeside scene in Kootenay National Park on the British Columbia-Alberta border just west of Banff.

(Left:) This browsing moose seems to be interrupting the business at hand to pose for its picture.

(Below:) Granite bluffs in Lighthouse Park, Point Atkinson, turn a soft yellow in the slanting light of the setting sun. The bluffs mark the southern end of British Columbia's Coast Mountains.

(Opposite:) Winter's touch fashions a forestscape of ethereal beauty as the white water of a stream vies for center stage with the snow-draped rocks and trees.

VANCOUVER ISLAND

V ancouver Island stretches north from the stormy waters of the Strait of Juan de Fuca, a vast landform more like a Pacific continent than an island. Early explorers often thought that this island (almost 300 miles long north-to-south, and the largest in western America) was the leading edge of the thousand-mile-long mainland coast range.

In recent geological history, Vancouver Island was in fact the western edge of Canada, a land mass connected along most of its length to the present mainland. This land (called Cascadia) sank to the ocean floor during violent upheavals of the Coast Range. Although only the mountain tops of Cascadia remained, Vancouver Island and the Queen Charlotte Islands to the north were created. To this day, the sinking of Cascadia is regarded by visitor and resident alike as an exceptional piece of natural good fortune.

In many respects, Vancouver Island is the epitome of the natural characteristics of British Columbia. Defined by Pacific waters, its shoreline granite carved into awesome forms by the eternal surf, the island boasts an immense sweep of fir and cedar forest that extends unbroken to the northern boundaries, except where high mountain peaks and glacial cols break through.

(Opposite:) The Myrtle River's Helmcken Falls, in Wells Gray Park, plung 475 feet into the volcanic gorge of Helmcken Canyon. The pool at the base of the falls is believed to be nearly as deep as the falls are high.

(Following Full Page:) Mt. Robson in the Rainbow Range is dazzling in her white robe of snow, with fleecy white clouds in attendance.

(Following Page, Above:) A summer sunset paints a fiery sky over the Gulf Islands, off Vancouver Island.

(Following Page, Below:) A field of dandelions sets off Bridge Lake in the Cariboo area.

This is the kind of place of which legends are made — and were made for centuries on the mythic architypical Indian totem poles. Later, western man created his own connection with this land: Sir Francis Drake, explorer under Queen Elizabeth I, sailed up the coast in 1579; the highest peak on the island is named for his ship, the *Golden Hind.* In 1778, Captain James Cook with shipmate George Vancouver sailed into Nootka (just off the island's west coast) to repair a mast. Fourteen years later, after circumnavigating the island, Captain George Vancouver claimed it for King George III. Impressed and awed by the wild beauty of the island, these early explorers (like the early totem carvers) wanted a personal and lasting identity with the land. Early maps abound with family names identifying spectacular mountains, rivers, and coastal areas: Vancouver, Quadra, Barkley, Douglas, and Strathcona have now become the geographic signposts of Vancouver Island.

Like the whole of B. C., Vancouver Island is defined by other measures than highways or roads, a certain indicator that it remains virtually untouched by modern technology. In modern terms, there are no real highways on the island, although there is one fairly good double-lane road along the southeastern coast, a short, somewhat poor, paved road on the southwest tip, and a paved-dirt-road combination traversing east-to-west at mid-island. Consequently, residents here (as in the entire province) are basically regionalists, and identify themselves in relation to a specific piece of geography. A Tofino resident is one who lives midway up the Island's west coast in a rainforest that is extremely rugged in winter. Conversely, a person from the Malahat lives in a climatically mild, east-coast mountain area.

There are four distinct regions on Vancouver Island, with the interior highlands forming the apex of each region. In the south, there are the low altitude land-plates that gradually become a level plateau on which the city of Victoria is built. The only urban center on the island, Victoria, with its English charm, has long been a favorite of all northern travelers. The provincial parliament, and most B. C. government agencies, are also located in Victoria. Although almost 20 per cent of the provincial population lives in this area, the fine park system gives the visitor a feeling of relatively open natural space.

Southwestern Vancouver Island, a distinct geographic area girded by the 64-mile-long road from Victoria to Port Renfrew, is basically an open-ocean region analogous to the Monterey-Big Sur area of 150 years ago. An emergent coastline, large geological stairsteps covered with moderately dense wind-twisted conifers and arbutus, pushes toward the interior highlands. The climate here is mild for B. C., with only intermittent snow during the winter. The town of Sooke, with some logging and fishing industry, is the only village before reaching Port Renfrew, the end of the road.

Again, Port Renfrew is a case of the architypical B. C. phenomenon of transportation routes being totally stopped by wilderness frontiers. A cursory view of any B. C. map will show that most roads dwindle off into dirt pathways or stop abruptly at natural obstacles. The way north here is by footpath, the renowned West Coast Trail that winds steeply through Pacific Rim Park, past spectacular Tsusint Falls where cascading tons of water fall directly onto the beach. The northern end of the trail, at Bamfield, can also be reached by car or boat from Port Alberni. The most popular and accessible portion of the west coast, at Long Beach and Tofino, can also be reached via Route 4 through the interior highlands. This road traverses the island's interior, passing through Cathedral Grove, the oldest stand of Douglas fir in B. C.

The most familiar region of Vancouver Island is the east coast, a narrow strip of land running northward between the calm tidal waters of Georgia Strait and the interior highlands. Beginning at Victoria, the highway bisects the Malahat (a rolling hill area resplendent with indigenous arbutus) with a clear view of the major Gulf Islands, and crosses several major rivers (Cowichan, Chemainus, Nanaimo, Englishman, Qualicum, Oyster, Campbell) as it follows the coast to Kelsey Bay and Port Hardy.

The feeling of open natural area still exists in this region. At any given point, a ten-minute walk from the highway will take the hiker into heavily timbered forests. The southern area was logged after the turn of the century, so most conifers are second growth, towering young giant cedars and firs. In the northern section work is still under way on tree farms, an enlightened approach to harvesting that ensures the availability of high quality trees, and a maturing cycle of only 25 years.

Although the eastern region has less than half the rainfall of the west coast, the rivers draining the high interior alpine area ensure excellent spawning conditions for salmon and steelhead, well-watered crops for the Comox Valley, and rapid timber growth on the tree farms. Campbell River, salmon capital of Canada, also provides access to the 561,179-acre Strathcona Provincial Park and icy Forbidden Plateau.

(Following Two Pages:) Entrance Peak, 7,550 feet, is near Meziadin Lake on the Stewart-Cassiar Highway in northwestern British Columbia. Behind these peaks lies the massive Cambria Icefield, 1,200 square miles in area.

Sections of the north island region are as remote and wild now as they were when first sighted by Captain Cook. Travel beyond Port Hardy is accomplished by logging roads that disappear into the oblivion of heavy forests. Large stands of Douglas fir and Sitka spruce, centuries old, remain forever inviolate and safe because of the rugged terrain. Except for a small turn-of-the-century attempt at settlement by Danish pioneers near Cape Scott, the north coast has always been pristine widlerness.

Vancouver Island, with its vast wilderness areas and few human settlements confined to narrow coast landstrips, is British Columbia in microcosm. Human settlers have been forced to accommodate themselves to the terrain. Incapable of dominating it with technology, they have evolved a way of life whereby a kind of natural harmony has emerged which will ensure its preservation.

THE COAST REGION

T he coast region, the southwestern edge of the British Columbia mainland, is an area of infinite variety and geographic change. Although Vancouver, a densely populated metropolitan city, is located here, much of the nearby natural landscape is as mountainous and primitive as anything found in the far north or Chilcotin-Cariboo. Conversely, the farmlands of the Fraser Valley are as gentle and well-tended as any on the continent. The Coast Region, uniquely surprising in its natural contrasts, remains one of the most appealing areas on the entire West Coast.

There are two outstanding geographic areas in the coast region: the jagged and precipitous Coast Range, and the Fraser River Delta lands. Without the mighty Fraser River cutting its 800-mile sweep to the sea, the entirety of the Fraser Delta and lower mainland would simply be the southern tip of the Coast Range.

The Fraser River has been a prime shaping force of this land. Hurtling with tremendous power through the narrow, precipitous gorges of the Fraser Canyon, this maelstrom of a river flattens out above Chilliwack, 80 miles east of Vancouver. This area is the central Fraser Valley, a lush farmland spread in wide rectangles along the river. From here, to the point where it meets the sea at Richmond, the Fraser flows through the rich delta soil of the valley.

(Following Page, Above:) Eagle Lake, a beautiful jewel in the Chilcotin area of the Coast Mountains, has waters of such transparent blue that details on the lake bottom are clearly visible 60 feet below the surface.

(Following Page, Below:) In the slanting light of the setting sun the jumbled mountains of Kootenay National Park look something like chocolate cake with vanilla frosting.

(Following Full Page:) Little Qualicum Falls tumbles down its intricate rocky stairstep on Vancouver Island's Qualicum River.

Most of the lower mainland, the Province's most populous area, is built on Fraser River Delta land. The city of Vancouver dominates the lower mainland, a metropolitan center with fine parks, excellent schools, and museums, and its own unique character. Located on the blue waters of Burrard Inlet, the city is framed on the north by the leading edge of the Coast Range. This mountain landscape gives Vancouver one of the most spectacular natural settings of any city in the world. The southern edges of Grouse, Seymour, and Hollyburn Mountains extend into Burrard Inlet. The sections adjacent to Vancouver are a watershed for the city, densely forested with cedar and unused to a surprising extent. A fine natural habitat, the watershed has large populations of black bear, raccoon, and blacktail deer.

Ten miles west, the Coast Range begins its spectacular, 1,000-mile sweep up the north coast. Glacier-carved, deep fjords penetrate up to 60 miles into the granite abutment. The effect is the creation of tidal, saltwater lakes that offer superb salmon fishing, and a coast landscape without parallel. The high peaks rise directly from the sea in rocky vertical expanses that dwarf passing boats or solitary hikers.

The most heavily used fjord is Howe Sound. Since the southern entrance is only a short drive from Vancouver, this has become the gateway to major outdoor recreation: Whistler Mountain, Garibaldi Park, The Chief, and Black Tusk all offer prime skiing, alpine climbing, and camping areas.

Except for the waterways of the Strait of Georgia, the only way north along the Coast Range is by a single two-lane road. This roadway requires two ferry crossings, at Howe Sound and Jervis Inlet, and close to six hours to travel its 90-mile length. However, it is along this byway that the true character of the coast emerges. The steep, sawtooth mountain ridge rises directly from the ocean. The heavy rainforest is so dense that even black bears use dirt roads and powerline cuts for travel. The underbush of blueberry, blackberry, salmonberry, and the thorny Devil's Club is often eight feet high, forming an impenetrable barrier.

The heavy Coast Range rainforest stands in green contrast to the bare-rock, glacial peaks. Alpine climbing expeditions are annually carried out in the Coast Range, especially near the Mount Waddington glacier. Thousands of feet below the shoreline twists northward around granite boulders and the tidal estuaries of countless streams and small rivers.

The town of Powell River, near road's-end at Lund, is the prime example of a Coast-Range habitation. Originally constructed as a "company town" decades ago by the forest industry, and still dependent on a pulp-paper mill as the primary industry, Powell River is a port town tied closely with all north coast and north island communities. All major travel and goods exchange is by boat because the rugged terrain of the Coast Range has defeated all attempts at major road building. Consequently, and fortunately, these north-coast communities have achieved a kind of harmonious accommodation with the natural environment, and a certain respect for the awesome natural power unleashed by winter storms.

The Coast Range is one of the most primitive alpine and forest regions in the world. Unsurpassed in natural beauty in summer, it is also unsurpassed for massive natural force during winter.

(Left:) Flowering Cacti are abundant in the ''desert'' areas of the Okanagan Valley, southern British Columbia.

(Below:) Garibaldi Lake, in Garibaldi Park, is situated on a basalt mesa 6,600 feet high called The Table. The lake was formed when lava from once-active Mt. Price (right) dammed a glacial creek. Mt. Garibaldi is on the left.

(Opposite:) The waters of Howe Sound, a few miles north of Vancouver, B.C., stir to movement under a sky filling with the clouds of an approaching storm.

SOUTHERN INTERIOR

A land of contrasts, the southern interior of British Columbia encompasses many dramatic extremes of the natural environment. Divided into two large regions — the Okanagan in the southwestern quadrant and the mountainous Kootenay in the southeast — this is the prime interior agricultural and outdoor recreational land of the province. Topographically, the southern interior covers the spectrum from cactus and sagebrush country to high alpine areas of wildflowers and permanent glacial ice. An immense land of more than 25 million acres, it holds massive reserves of fresh water in the Kamloops, Shuswap, and Okanagan Lakes, and the Thompson and Columbia Rivers.

The Okanagan Region, often called the fruit basket of western Canada, still remains an area of striking natural landscape. Central Okanagan, the Vernon-Kelowna-Penticton lake district, is the agricultural heartland. With a mild, dry climate and a Mediterranean chaparral terrain of conifers and grasslands, this well-watered region with its rich soil yields bountiful harvests of delicious peaches, apples, and plums.

The long shores of Okanagan Lake provide exceptional water recreational opportunities, and a sometimes-welcome, warm holiday respite for the snow-bound residents of northern British Columbia. The most appealing aspect of the Okanagan to British Columbians is its unusual climate, atypical of the province as a whole, and very likely a dream in southern California. An economic and psychological bonanza in a country of harsh winter realities and arctic winds, this region is the symbol of summertime.

Away from the lake area, the landscape assumes a different, more typically British Columbia tone. On the western Okanagan borders, near Cache Creek and Merritt, a northern desert and chaparral area dominates: high temperatures, with hot winds constantly eroding barren cliff faces, and only the Thompson River offering visual relief.

(Preceding Page:) Silver Skagit Falls tumbles down a cobbled rock face into Silver Lake River in the Skagit Valley.

(Opposite:) A late afternoon sun highlights the tide pools of the rock shelf near Port Renfrew on Vancouver Island.

(Right:) The brilliant red of the wild rose is admirably set off by the plant's foliage.

(Below:) The Golden Ears, rugged sentinels of Golden Ears Parks north of Vancouver, overlook this forest scene.

(Following Page, Above:) Long Beach, Vancouver Island.

(Following Page, Below:) Sunset turns the sky a brilliant gold and etches the tortured profile of Mt. Goodsir in Kootenay National Park.

(Preceding Page:) These aspens in Coldwater Valley near Princeton are beginning to take on their autumn colors.

(Left:) Chocolate lily, Indian paintbrush, and other wildflowers make a lavish showing in Botanie Valley, near Lytton.

(Below:) Winter snow scene, Apex Mountain Park, near Penticton.

(Opposite:) A Stanley Park scene in Vancouver.

(Following Two Pages:) Mountains and trees and water combine in this pleasant autumn scene in the Skagit Valley.

(Opposite:) Lava Lake lies calmly within its forested banks near Terrace. Oscar Peak shoulders up in the background.

(Right:) Three mountain goats — mama and her two kids — hold still for a family portrait.

(Below:) Spetch Creek, near Mount Currie in the Pemberton Valley, looks like spun sugar as it tumbles between and around the red granite boulders lining its course. The streamside trees are red alder and western red cedar.

(Following Page, Above:) Black Tusk cinder cones add their own grotesque beauty to Garibaldi Park, north of Vancouver.

(Following Page, Below:) Kennedy Lake, near Long Beach on Vancouver Island, nestles serenely in the embrace of its forested lava banks.

(Preceding Page, Above:) This jumble of lush growth is typical of the rain forests of the Coast Mountains.

(Preceding Page, Below:) The Robson River and Mt. Robson team up for a beautiful wilderness setting in Mt. Robson Park, on the border of British Columbia and Alberta.

(Left:) The cloud sheathed mountainside in the background lends emphasis to the delicate pink of the wildflowers in the Kootenay Mountains near Nakusp.

(Below:) September brings changes to Silvermere Lake, near Ruskin in the Lower Fraser Valley.

(Opposite:) This winter forest scene in the Garibaldi Nature Conservancy Area epitomizes nature's delicate handiwork. Mt. Garibaldi is seen through the trees.

Farther east, the prosperous town of Kamloops stretches into rolling ranchland. David Stuart's Overlanders ended their historic raft journey here in 1867. Now, Kamloops, a major trade center, concentrates on cattle-raising in a mixed grassland-forest area that abounds with wildlife, and ties them closely with the Chilcotin-Cariboo region to the north. Some of the best rainbow trout fishing in the world occurs within a 50-mile radius of Kamloops. Directly east of Kamloops, the town of Salmon Arm marks the northeast border of the Okanagan on the shores of the 125-square-mile Shuswap Lake. The landscape alternates between rolling maple- and fir-covered foothills and wide level valleys. The main spawning ground for the world's population of sockeye salmon is the Adams River, only a short drive from the townsite.

The second major region of the southern interior is the Kootenay area, the entire southeastern quadrant of British Columbia. Easily one of the most spectacular mountain regions of the continent, this area contains the highest interior peaks (including Mt. Robson, highest in the Rocky Mountains), major forest and alpine areas, and an exceedingly heavy winter snowfall.

The Kootenay region encompasses two major mountain systems, the Rockies and the Selkirks. Within the Rockies, an ancient range of uplifted sedimentary geologic plates bent and twisted into awesome forms, the Selkirk Range has pushed its granite ridge up through the west-slope rock crust. The effect is similar to a row of planted seedlings breaking through the topsoil — a new, young mountain range has seemingly grown from the old range. The

(Opposite:) This stream and its moss-covered rocks are near Mile 477, Alaska Highway, northern British Columbia.

(Following Page, Above:) The calm surface of this headwater lake and the surrounding dense forest create a mood of tranquility near Peachland.

(Following Page, Below:) Clearwater Valley in Wells Gray Park is decked out in blue-green finery as it sweeps up from the river.

(Following Full Page:) Sunset imparts a bronze hue to this setting on Pender Island, one of the Gulf Islands.

Tete Jaune Revelstoke-Monashee-Nelson region is a classic west-slope natural environment. Much wetter and more heavily forested than Alberta's Rockies, the Selkirks add a kind of new energy to the older mountain range. The Columbia River Valley dominates a series of high-slope valleys that support some agriculture and grazing lands. Often, a few horses or cattle can be seen in green fields dwarfed by spectacular background peaks. The town of Golden, picturesque beside the Kicking Horse River and the Selkirks, could easily be located in the Alps. This village has a living historical connection with the mountains: several Swiss guides and mountaineers, brought to British Columbia by the Canadian Pacific Railway as local regional explorers, have retired in Golden. Most of high peaks here were first conquered by those mountaineers almost four decades ago. From Golden, as from virtually all the Kootenay towns, the landscape is awesome: rock- and ice-covered craigs, forests of cedar, spruce, and larch at lower altitudes, and the always present evidence of massive rockslides. With over 30 major peaks, and several active glaciers, the mountainscape is superabundantly alpine. The single most prominent peak is Mt. Robson. Although no more spectacular than the Bugaboos, Yoho, or Mt. Asiniboine, it has the distinction of being the highest peak in the Canadian Rockies. Spring and summer, alpinists try their luck and skill on the hazardous ice and rock bands of Mt. Robson's vertical face.

With the exception of a few National Park village areas, the Kootenay alpine regions remain in their wilderness state. Here, as on the north coast and Vancouver Island, civilization has accommodated itself to nature's dictates. A prime summer recreation area, the mountains are mainly seen from passing car windows, and walked on only by experienced and expert mountaineers.

CHILCOTIN— CARIBOO

The Chilcotin-Cariboo is an immense land mass encompassing the entire central interior of British Columbia. Defined on the west and east by the major Coast and Rocky Mountain ranges, respectively, the region is typically arid desert in the southern areas around Cache Creek, an extreme contrast to the rainforest and heavy snowfields of northern Tweedsmuir Park. This is basically a high plateau country, although high-altitude mountain areas exist both east and west. But the great stretch of land is in the thousands of square miles of rolling hills, marshland, lakes, and stands of aspen, cedar, and fir that blanket mountain slopes and riverbanks.

The Chilcotin-Cariboo is the frontier, a land close to the dreams of the Old West. Cattle raising is the chief business here, with provincial grazelands leased by the thousand acres. The borders of some ranches cannot be reached in two days travel. The land seems immense, the sky often bright and horizon-wide; and, for the ranchers, it's a very rugged winter life.

The Chilcotin Region is the western interior quadrant. The Coast Range and the Fraser River define the west-east boundaries, the desert areas of Cache Creek mark the south. The northern borderline has always been indefinite, although the Prince George—Prince Rupert highway seems acceptable to most of these frontier residents. Except for air travel, the only way into the Chilcotin is via the Williams Lake—Bella Coola road (Highway 20). In 1793, Alexander MacKenzie first crossed this area in his famed continental traverse. When he reached Bella Coola, he became the first explorer to cross the country overland. Even today, this route is sometimes hazardous and, in some seasons, impossible.

(Following Two Pages:) This lonely wilderness panorama was photographed north of Ross Lake, looking south, in the Skagit Valley.

The entrance to the Chilcotin from Williams Lake (south of Prince George) is through interminable miles of hill region, grazelands, and partially cleared forest slopes. The ranchers and the loggers engage in old-time western feuds here: it takes more than 100 acres of forest-land to support one cow and calf, and by law the forest industry must replant the cut areas: the ranchers want the entire area as grassland.

A large portion of the region, from Puntzi, Kleena Kleene, Nimpo, and Anahim lakes, is similar to the classic steppe regions of Idaho, Wyoming, and eastern Africa. Clear bright-sky nights, a huge wildlife and migratory bird population, marshland and lakes make this a rich region for naturalists. The surrounding mountain peaks are covered with a perpetual snowpack, and often the alpine areas receive 40 feet of new snow every winter.

The road from Anahim Lake west crosses the southern section of Tweedsmuir Provincial Park, the largest in British Columbia. Tweedsmuir offers a magnificent variety of natural habitat: desert areas, high alpine peaks and meadows, active glaciers, and two of the best salmon-steelhead rivers in the world. The wildlife is bountiful and includes almost every northern species — and a large population of grizzly bear.

North coast mountain region, interior plateau, and steppe, the very expanse of land ensures and perpetuates the wild frontier nature of the Chilcotin.

The Cariboo Region is similar, although less frontier-like in character, to the Chilcotin. The mountainous region is on the eastern slope here, and the western border shares the same rolling ranchland with the Chilcotin. The Prince George—Tete Jaune Highway defines the north border, and the Cache Creek — Salmon Arm section of Trans-Canada Highway marks the southern extremes of this region.

Towns, and signs of rural habitation are much more frequent in this central interior region, and cattle, lumber, and small farms along the North Thompson River share common land with deer, moose, and bear. However, despite the presence of people and industry, the land and forests of western spruce and fir of the Cariboo remain reasonably open and natural.

Since the lower portions of the Cariboo are only a six-hour drive from Vancouver, heavy recreational pressure is placed on localized areas. A prime fishing and hunting locale, with close to 300 resident guides, the hills and lakes around Kamloops, the 100-mile House-Little Fort crossing, and the canoe routes of Bowron Lakes all show signs of too much human crowding. At mid-summer this area and Garibaldi Park on the coast resemble a California State Park. Fortunately, this phenomenon is still confined to small localized areas of the province. And, both the immense land mass available and pattern charts of recreation-al land use indicate that such over-use will occur (or continue) in less than a half-dozen isolated areas.

The northern border of the Cariboo, from Prince George to Tete Jaune, cuts into an increasingly mountainous area. Following the Fraser River drainage through Yellowhead Pass, the area is almost entirely a black spruce interior forest. Although this area often experiences difficult winters, there is a certain surprising ease to the land here — a comfortable respite from the more rugged climes, both coast and rockies.

The natural landscape is transformed into a more traditional British Columbia scene along the primary north-south route from Kamloops to Tete Jaune. The ranchlands of the Kamloops area become more heavily forested on the trip north. Ice- and snow-armored peaks, the leading high edge of the Rockies, become almost overpowering in their massive thrust.

True mountain wilderness, and alpine regions similar to the Kootenays, dominate the landscape at Blue River and the 1.8 million-acre Wells Gray Park. An outstanding primitive area, Wells Gray Park is one of British Columbia's best kept wilderness secrets. Access is limited intentionally, although there is a reasonably good trail system. Alpine meadows, permanent snowfields, active glaciers, and unique lava beds combine with spectacular woodlands in rare natural beauty. Flowing streams and lake water are seemingly everywhere, and there are a full dozen awesome waterfalls.

The tremendous mountain regions of Wells Gray and Tweedsmuir and the vast rolling landscape of the central interior all combine to make the Chilcotin-Cariboo a land of infinite variety and wilderness frontier. The immense physical space and open sky place this region on the outer edge of human comprehension.

(Following Page, Above, Left:) Pinto Lake, in the Chilcotin area of the Coast Mountains.

(Following Page, Lower Left:) The mighty Peace River Valley is a majestic sight at Bear Flat, near Fort St. John.

(Following Page, Above, Right:) The milky blue-green waters of the Chilcotin River are seen here near Alexis Creek. The river flows from glacier-fed Chilco Lake.

(Following Page, Below, Right:) Hat Creek Valley, looking west toward Marble Canyon.

FAR NORTH

The far north is another vast land, unexpected and surprising to the traveller accustomed to the dense forests of tall cedars and the alpine areas of lower latitudes. Not that there are no mountains: Mt. Fairweather, in the northwest corner of the province, is Canada's highest. Yet, the predominant feeling one experiences in the north is of relative flatness, of never-ending thousands of square miles once buried under tons of glacial ice.

Despite the recent rush toward northern oil, with pipelines and rail routes, and the faulty understanding of ecological balances in the north, modern technology seems insignificant and toy-like, lost in the expanse of land. In fact, the present industrial involvement is not much different from the 1870 gold rush to the Stikine River. At that time, there were so many miners and prospectors entering the area that a railway had to be built into Atlin-Discovery. However, the land exacted its toll: all that remmains are decaying sluices and cabins.

The north is too large and unknown to be either comprehended or even seriously exploited by present industrial technology. For example, the major transportation highway routes are only gravel roadways, sections of which are impossible to travel during the spring-breakup. From the air, these roads look like trails hacked through primitive wilderness. In reality, the roads are limited to serving the same basic needs that former trail systems served: a simple movement of goods and people, with virtually no recognition of the land as anything except a physical obstacle. Consequently, except for the two or three ribbons of gravel roadway and a few townsites, the land remains exactly as it has been for the last 10,000 years.

Remoteness is the most important environmental factor protecting the land from civilization. Regardless of where a local resident or traveler is in the north, he feels as if he is a very long way away from anything else (although, perhaps, fairly close to the northern end of the world). Car drives of 600-800 miles are considered short, and air service is used as commonly as urban bus rides. Still, there is no way to compress that vast remoteness, and residents usually stay in their own large regions.

The two main regions of the far north, west, and interior east are as different from one another as New York City and the far side of the moon. The interior east is bisected by Highway 97 (the northern 600 miles is the Alaska Highway) which tentatively pushes through the Peace River area, and is the primary route between the towns of Dawson Creek, Fort St. John, Fort Nelson and the Yukon border at Lower Post.

In the summer, northern daylight lasts more than 20 hours in this usually sunny area. Surprisingly, much of this northern bushland and hill region has been turned into a prime agricultural area for grain and wheat production, especially around Dawson Creek. Energy from the generators at the Bennett Dam supply power to most of the province.

The landscape is more heavily forested, with dense stands of spruce, near Fort St. John — the oldest town in B. C., originally settled by Alexander Mackenzie. The terrain requires strenuous hiking, and careful use of the numerous lakes and streams. In Fort Nelson, the flat landscape is deceptive because the wilderness edge extends into the village itself. Wildlife is plentiful, including the carnivores: timber wolf, lynx, grizzly, and wolverine all exact a certain degree of respect when a hiker walks into their piece of the woods.

From Fort Nelson, the road cuts its final slice through the interior east, passing through the exceptional northern landscape of Stone Mountain Park with bare rock peaks and stunted conifers offering dramatic proof of the natural permanence of this region. Near the Yukon border and the northern tip of this region, after endless miles of scrub pine, spruce, and muskeg, the land seems open and forever.

The west region, a basically coastal area of the far north, stands in striking contrast to the interior east. The highest, most rugged mountains of the province, tremendous glaciers and icefields, and lush, dense forests of pine, aspen, spruce, and cottonwood combine to create a wilderness area unsurpassed in beauty. Easily the most rugged area in North America, this region holds its natural wonders like treasures that must be discovered by intrepid explorers: the deep flowing Stikine River, the skyblue ice of Bear Glacier, the lava cones of Edziza and the parklands of Spatsizi. These are indeed wilderness treaures, received only after determined travel.

(Left:) A black bear, apparently disapproving of having his photograph taken, has retreated into the treetops.

(Below:) This primeval rain forest is in Cathedral Grove Park near Port Alberni, Vancouver Island. The massive western red cedar and fir trees that grow in this area of 180 inches of rainfall annually are nearly 2,000 years old. Moss, sword fern, vanilla leaf, and Oregon grape thrive on the forest floor.

(Opposite:) Bear Glacier and Cambria Icefield in the Coast Mountains near Stewart are located in the most heavily glaciated region of Canada. The area receives more than 1,100 inches of snowfall during winter. The glacier icefall here is more than 150 feet high.

The principal route between Prince Rupert, Stewart and Cassiar bisects the interior west. A difficult road to travel, it runs through virtually untouched primitive wilderness for over 400 miles. At Stewart, the road is practically on the Alaska border, north of Ketchikan. At this point, access to Bear Glacier is usually possible. Ice at the glacier toe is 150 feet thick. Compressed for over 600 years by tons of pressure, the entire face reflects blue color. The ice has actually changed its molecular structure under the constant pressure and is incredibly hard.

North from Bear Glacier are the Stikine Plateau, Dease Lake, and the volcanic region of Edziza, scene of the province's most recent volcanic eruptions. From this point north to Cassiar and east to Spatsizi, the wilderness is often impenetrable. A primitive area, it supports an exceptionally large wildlife population which includes almost every large animal in the province.

Atlin, west of Cassiar and north of Juneau, Alaska, and the most northern town in B.C., is on the shore of Atlin Lake, largest lake in the province (300 square miles). The mountains in this area are 17,000-19,000 feet high, glacier scoured, and formidable. Atlin provincial Park (more than 575,000 acres) contains Llewellyn Glacier, and one of the largest icefields on the continents.

Ice, high peaks, forest ground cover — the Far North region is primitive, wild, and exceptionally beautiful.